CREDIT CHAMPION

A Practical Guide to Leveraging Your Wealth and Increasing Your Purchasing Power

SYVOSKIA BRAY POPE

Credit Champion: A Practical Guide to Leveraging Your Wealth and Increasing Your Purchasing Power

ISBN 978-0-578-71307-6

2020-First Edition

Printed in the United States of America

TABLE OF CONTENTS

INTRODUCTION

Starting the Credit Conversation—Fixing Your Credit Character

"The best person to 'face' the problem is also the best person to 'fix' the problem—that is you!"
–Scott and Alison Hilton, authors of
The Credit Repair Book: The Credit Repair Company's Secret Weapon

Have you ever heard the saying, "You will never fix what you will never face?" Sadly, millions of people avoid implementing improvement strategies to fix their credit problems. They would rather jeopardize their credit character instead of fixing it. Many prefer to become credit culprits as opposed to being credit champions. My purpose for writing this workbook is because I am passionate about helping as many people as I can to become credit champions.

I do not sit in a seat of credit judgment or criticism. Throughout this book, I share the credit challenges I have experienced. I understand being deep in debt. I know what it is like to have a spouse die unexpectedly and face debt and expenses reducing from a two-person to a one-person income. Yet, I want you to realize that no matter how low your credit score, regardless of how deep in debt you are, despite how damaging your credit history may be, **YOU CAN BECOME A CREDIT CHAMPION!**

To begin the credit conversation, so you can begin your journey to becoming a credit champion, let's review some startling credit statistics.

- About 30% of Americans have poor or bad credit scores, www.foxbusiness.com.
- One in every eight Americans is completely unaware of their current credit score, www.nypost.com.
- The NFCC study found that 36% of people think there's no reason to check their credit score. About 8% didn't know how to, and another 8% thought it was too expensive, www.creditdonkey.com.

- 44% of consumers believe credit scores and credit reports mean the same thing, www.creditdonkey.com.
- 41% of Americans do not understand that a credit score measures your risk of not paying a loan, www.creditdonkey.com.
- The amount of credit card debt outstanding rose nearly three-fold between 1990 and 2002, from $173 billion to $661 billion, www.factretriever.com/credit-score-facts.
- On average, African-American and Latino households have worse credit scores than white households, www.factretriever.com/credit-score-facts.

Why do most people avoid engaging in a conversation about credit, let alone procrastinate about fixing their credit score? I have narrowed down 10 reasons people fear working on fixing their credit:

1. Pride
2. Impatient
3. Misinformed
4. Mistrust of financial experts
5. Afraid of seeking expert help
6. Fear of facing their past financial mistakes
7. Refusal to give up their poor spending habits
8. Too much debt, collections, and repossessions
9. Do not have the financial knowledge or financial means
10. Poor generational core values revolving around finances and spending

The 3 Attributes of A Credit Champion

Becoming a credit champion is not a sprint of quick fixes so you can reach an imaginary finish line of temporary change. Becoming a credit champion requires a persistent journey of endurance to a changed lifestyle that leads to achieving the financial goals you have set for yourself. Much like many of the athletes who are standout winners in their respective fields, becoming a credit champion will require three unwavering attributes.

The first attribute is having unyielding determination. Determination is *the ability to continue trying to do something, although it is very difficult.* When you think of the concept of determination, you may think of the 1930s children's story entitled *The Little Engine That Could.* Let me share a quick synopsis of the story to illustrate credit champion determination.

The story centers on a large train that must receive help to make it over a high mountain after its engine breaks down. During the train's dilemma, many trains are able, yet not willing, to pull the train over the mountain. The trains that are the obvious choices to help the large train out of a jam refuses. However, a smaller blue engine comes along and, although it does not have the apparent ability to help, the key is that the little blue engine has the will to try.

Not only is the little blue engine willing, but it has determination. The blue train gives the endeavor all of its strength to offer support for the large engine. The determination is overtly apparent by the blue engine's continuous chant, *"I think I can. I think I can."*

Successful credit champions think, speak, and do what is necessary to reach their financial destination. For credit champions, the determination to reach their credit goals begins with progressive thoughts, proceeds to positive mantras, and ends with persistent actions. Remember, as General Colin Powell once quoted, *"A dream doesn't become reality through magic; it takes sweat, determination, and hard work."*

The second trait of a credit champion is discipline. Discipline involves *training that makes you willing to obey or control yourself.* President Abraham Lincoln defined that *"Discipline is choosing between what you want now and what you want most."* Sadly, though, there are a growing number of people who live for their superficial financial now, instead of working toward a solvent financial future. Credit champions plan for the now and the next.

Please understand that discipline requires blood, sweat, and tears. It is not easy. It will be painful. However, ask yourself, *"Is fixing my credit to leverage my wealth and increase my purchasing power worth temporary uneasiness if I will eventually reach lasting financial wellness?"* The answer should be a resounding and continuous, *"Yes!"*

The last attribute of a credit champion is dedication. When dedicated, you effortlessly have the *willingness to give a lot of time and energy to something because it is important.* Dedication is an unwavering focus to manifest your goal. It is having unstoppable perseverance to reach your goal. Credit champions dedicate their time to analyzing their spending habits and financial views that contributed to their credit struggles.

Throughout this interactive workbook, I will help you become a credit champion by helping you to:

- Debunk all of your credit myths and misunderstandings.
- Negotiate with your creditors without fear, shame, or guilt.

- Develop a spending budget that is realistic and relevant to your financial goals.
- Bounce back into a positive credit flow, despite the death of a spouse, divorce, or damaging spending habits.

Before you begin your journey, please understand that credit champions are not born. They are nurtured and developed. Despite poor or unhealthy financial habits, you can grow from being a credit culprit guilty of not paying your bills on time, contributing to negative credit history to becoming a credit champion.

Your credit score comprises three digits that you should not ignore. You can lie about these three digits. You can misunderstand these three digits. However, the great thing about these three digits is that you can repair them. Remember, your credit score can cultivate the credit champion within you.

It is my goal that you become a model credit champion. I will explore all aspects that can negatively affect your credit and ultimately your financial wealth and purchasing power. High debt decreases your cash flow. Not paying your bills on time blemishes your credit history. Ignoring debt collectors pushes you into a financial position you could have avoided had you been proactive.

By the end of ***Credit Champion: A Practical Guide to Leveraging Your Wealth and Increasing Your Purchasing Power***, you will know the importance of having a healthy credit score and working diligently to sustain it. Throughout this book, your entire money mindset will shift from operating in a deficit to living in a financial surplus. This transformation takes time and hard work.

The benefits of implementing the tips and strategies within this book will unleash the credit champion within you. You shall have the essential secrets for creating a winning lifestyle of holistic financial wealth and wellness. Ready? Set? Let's unleash the credit champion within you.

CHAPTER SELF-CHECK: In the space below, choose someone you admire as a champion. Explain how they embody the three attributes of a champion discussed above. Describe, in detail, how you can apply the attributes to becoming a credit champion.

SECTION 1:

CREDIT EDUCATION

"Education is the most powerful weapon which you can use to change the world."
– Nelson Mandela

Education is power! Power to change. Power to live in peace. Power to build and expand. Power to influence and transform society. When you know better, you will always do better. So, education is definitely power.

Credit education is even more powerful, both individually and collectively. When you know genuine facts about credit, you develop a lifestyle of leveraging your wealth and increasing your purchasing power. Credit education is not only powerful, it is pivotal to your financial peace and prosperity.

By the end of the chapters in this section, you will learn:

- ***The definition of your credit and an explanation of what your credit score is.***
- ***Why credit really matters in your personal and professional life.***
- ***How to debunk credit myths and uncover credit truths that credit agencies do not want you to know.***
- ***How to change your negative credit mindset that has been messing up your financial wellness.***

Remember, education is power. However, credit education is a powerful and persuasive weapon that destroys generational cycles of poverty, negative financial mindsets, and unproductive spending habits. Are you ready to become a credit champion? Then be open to learning and unlearning information about credit.

CHAPTER 1

Credit: What's It Really All About?

"If you don't take good care of your credit, then your credit won't take good care of you."
– Tyler Gregory

Credit score. Two simple words that, if not thoroughly understood, can create a chaotic life. Credit score. The three digits that can become an invisible thief to your financial peace and prosperity. Credit score. What is it really all about?

Before I explain the components of your credit score, I must give you a clear understanding of what credit is. Credit is the ability to receive goods and services before you render payment. It is an asset that keeps a record of paying back loans, credit cards, and other debt. Credit is trust between the **creditor** *(the person extending the credit)* and the **creditee** *(the person receiving the credit)* to obtain goods or services before payment, based on the trust that the creditee will make payment in the future.

Credit is your ability to make consistent payments over a period of time. The record of the timeliness of your payments that creditors report to **credit agencies** *(companies that collect information relating to the credit ratings of individuals and makes it available)* is your **credit history**. Your credit history creates a **credit score** that becomes a snapshot of your creditworthiness.

In a nutshell, receiving credit is an opportunity for the lender to loan you funds. The amount of credit you receive will eventually expand your credit collateral and develop your credit character. Your creditor bases its decision solely on the range of your credit score. **(Note: I will identify the score ranges between a good and poor credit score in another chapter.)**

Remember, the key to leveraging your wealth and increasing your purchasing power is to have a high credit score. Your high credit score shows creditors that you are a low credit risk. However, a low credit score shows creditors that you are a high credit risk.

Having a healthy credit score allows you to accomplish two critical goals. First, the better your credit score is, the better chance you have to leverage your current and future wealth. (Note: Throughout this book, wealth means economic wealth.)

Wealth is the total of your money, property, and other tangible possessions that you can exchange for monetary value. Wealth is having a substantial amount of goods and resources that have exchangeable value that you can use. Wealth is the accumulation of your assets, less your expenses.

What is leveraging your wealth? Leverage can be an intimidating word. However, it does not have to give you anxiety. To leverage wealth means to use your influence to obtain your desired goals. It means to use what you already have to get something better. Simply put, leveraging your wealth means to use your money, property, and other possessions to get more money, property, and possessions. (Note: In a later chapter, I will discuss, in further detail, the keys to obtain more of it).

CHAPTER SELF-CHECK: To assess your comprehension of the new terms in this section, complete the matching exercise.

1. ______ the person extending credita. credit
2. ______ a record of timeliness of your b. creditee
   payments made to credit lendersc. credit score
3. ______the person receiving creditd. creditor
4. ______ a snapshot of your creditworthinesse. credit history
5. ______your ability to make consistent payments
over a period of time

a. credit
b. creditee
c. credit score
d. creditor
e. creditor hisotry

CHAPTER 2

Why Does Credit Really Matter?

Your credit report and credit score are two of the most vital aspects of your financial health."
–Erin Lowry

Credit, specifically good credit, truly does matter in your life. As Erin Lowry quoted, *"Your credit report and credit score are two of the most vital aspects of your financial wealth."* I want to extend this quote. Having a favorable credit report, and maintaining a good credit score, is critical to your financial wealth and wellness. Simply put, credit matters because it has a direct impact on every facet of your life.

Good credit is your leverage to making big moves in your life. When your credit is in an acceptable range, you can do certain life activities with ease. Some of these activities include purchasing a car, buying a home, having the funding for your business idea, receiving loans and lines of credit at a lower interest rate, and improving your employment opportunities.

Some individuals believe credit equates to debt, and debt is bad. On the contrary, debt is not bad. It is the way you manage your debt that affects your credit history. Based on how you pay your bills, you have complete authority whether you are going to build a good credit history or a bad one.

Like building a career, building credit takes time, intentionality, and guidance from a credit coach. The first step in your credit journey is to acquire credit. First-time applicants must have three things when seeking credit.

First, have a steady **active** income. Active income, also known as **earned** income, is income received in exchange for performing a service. Examples of active income are wages, tips, salaries, and commissions.

Creditors may also look at your **passive** income. This is income you receive from assets you already have that generate revenue. Examples of passive income include rental property, royalties from intellectual property, and business income.

The last type of income is **portfolio** income. This is money you receive from selling an investment at a higher price than you paid for it. Investments such as stocks, bonds, and real estate are types of portfolio income.

However, lenders heavily examine the active income you have because it shows that you have a constant flow of cash to pay your debt. It is difficult to repay monies loaned to you if you do not have a flow of money consistently coming in. Credit champions know that to leverage wealth and increase purchasing power, their consistent cash flow speaks volumes to lenders.

The second step in obtaining credit is to show you can repay your debt on time. Even with credit cards, keep your balances low and pay them in a timely fashion. The third step is not to overextend yourself when you apply for credit. Do not ask for too much that is out of your budget **(I will discuss budgeting later in the book)**.

After you get credit, it is imperative for you to strive to build a good credit history. Much like anything else in life, the way you start a thing is usually the way you continue to do a thing. Even if you fall on unexpected hard financial times, your credit history does not have to be in jeopardy if you communicate and negotiate payments.

Getting credit is usually easier than building it. Below are some simple tips for maintaining good credit that www.wellsfargo.com shares:

- Pay bills on time.
- Check your credit history often.
- Keep long-standing accounts open.
- Keep your credit card balances low.
- Avoid applying for too many credit cards.
- Create a budget and stick to it no matter what.
- Schedule automatic payments or payment alerts.
- If you can pay more than your minimum balance, do so.

If you hit a financial bump that robs you of your positive credit history, you can rebuild. It is not the end of the world if you have to rebuild your credit. You must be proactive with your creditors. Let them know when you are in a financial crisis then apply the same strategies listed above for building your credit. Most lenders prefer to work with you instead of putting you in collection status.

As a developing credit champion, you must know that the matters of credit does matter. Remember that credit is not bad. However, if you mismanage your credit, you can create a bad credit history and a bad credit score. Yet, when you manage credit properly, it can bless your life.

CHAPTER ACTIVITY: Review the bulleted list on how to build your credit. You can also implement these strategies when you are striving to rebuild your credit. Whether you are building or rebuilding your credit, identify the strategy you will implement in the next thirty days.

After monitoring your activity for sixty days, return to your list to write a brief reflection describing the impact this strategy has made on your financial wellness.

CHAPTER 3

Credit Myths: Truths That They Really Don't Want You to Know

"Your mind doesn't know the difference between reality and fantasy. Your mind acts on what you feed it. Feed it good thoughts."
–Zig Ziglar

Sadly, we live in a society in which so-called "reality television" has shaped many people's desires, aspirations, and lifestyles. Many would rather keep up with the Kardashians than keep up with their credit score. Some prefer to search for houses such as those the agents show on *Million Dollar Listing*, instead of adhering to their thousandaire financial budget and cash flow. Unfortunately, the fantasy of the lives of people on "reality television" has become the distorted superficial lifestyle that incorporates high debt, low credit scores, and an even bleaker financial future.

Guru Zig Ziglar quoted that the only difference between your authentic reality and a fabricated fantasy you are living as your so-called reality results from what you feed your mind. When I reflect on my previous financial struggles and those of my clients, we did not directly or intentionally cope with the reality of our finances in a timely manner. As a result, rebuilding our credit became an important focus.

Yet, during the beginning phase of credit rebuilding when assisting my clients, they embraced many myths. A **myth** is a widely held belief or idea that is false. When you are striving to become a credit champion, you must debunk and dismiss the credit myths you have internalized. I will identify and discuss some of these myths in the rest of this chapter. Please note: this list is not an exhaustive list of credit myths. As you read, reflect on which myth you believe as reality.

CREDIT MYTH: Credit Agencies Have Legal Authority Over What Is on Your Report and When and How You See It

This is false. Credit agencies have no legal authority to suggest credit decisions, nor do they control what is or is not on your credit report. However, federal and state laws regular credit bureaus to ensure people are not being abused or damaged by agency practices.

According to www.creditagencies.uslegal.com, credit agencies are limited by the Fair Credit Reporting Act (FCR Act). This Act sets the following limitations:

- **The type of information credit reporting agencies may compile.**
- **The manner in which information may be reported.**
- **The procedures for ensuring the accuracy of the information.**

The primary purpose of credit agencies is to obtain and deliver information concerning your creditworthiness. They have no legal authority to deny or make lending decisions. The only job of credit agencies is to report the information accurately that your lenders send them.

CREDIT MYTH: Credit Agencies Have A Legal Obligation to Report All Information About You on Your Credit Report

Not true. Understand that laws do not require credit agencies to put anything on your credit report. Agencies have a duty to report accurately what lenders send them. However, they can only report the information that lenders, with whom you have an account, send them.

CREDIT MYTH: Everything Reported on Your Credit Report Is Accurate and You Can Not Dispute or Remove It

Absolutely not! That is why credit champions are intentional about monitoring their credit reports. Humans make errors in compiling and sending information. When you discover something is not accurate, it is your right to dispute it so they can remove it. You can dispute with the credit bureau or directly with your creditor.

When disputing with the credit bureau, they must investigate your dispute with the business you have the allegation against. Once the investigation is complete, if changes are warranted because the information is incorrect or cannot be verified, the credit agency is required to correct your report. Everything in your report is **not** always correct.

CREDIT MYTH: Despite Your Previous Negative Payment History, You Can Change Your Not-So-Good Payment History or Erase It If You Paid the Past Due Balance in Full

This is also incorrect. Paying off your debt is a good thing, especially if the debt is categorized as a collection account. However, paying the debt does not erase your negative credit history. Activities such as bankruptcies, collection accounts, discharges as well as untimely payments are on your report. These activities can remain on your report for up to seven to ten years.

CREDIT MYTH: Credit Inquiries Do Not Negatively Impact My Credit Score

Let's put this into the correct context. There are two types of credit inquiries: soft and hard inquiries. A soft inquiry is exactly what it sounds like. This manner of inquiry is delicate and impacts nothing. According to www.myfico.com, examples of soft inquiries are you personally checking your credit report, an employer requesting your credit report for an employment screening or your bank getting your report for a customer credit quality check.

On the other hand, hard inquiries can affect your credit score. Hard inquiries are a part of the qualifying process for installment loans, mortgages, and credit cards to determine your creditworthiness to the lender from whom you are seeking service.

Too many inquiries in a short period of time can negatively impact your score. How much hard inquiries impact your score depends on the person's credit history. In a nutshell, soft inquiries do not negatively impact your credit score. Conversely, hard inquiries can decrease your credit score depending on the number of inquiries in a short period of time, as well as the person's credit history.

There are many other credit myths. Below are some credit myths listed on www.moneycrashers.com and www.experian.com:

1) **All debt is the same type of debt:** All debt is very different. For instance, a $75,000 revolving credit card balance is totally different from a $75,000 mortgage balance. The mortgage balance is a part of wealth creation. The mortgage debt is a lasting stable asset that appreciates. On the other hand, the revolving credit balance of the same amount is decreasing your purchasing power because credit card debt is a vanishing, tangible asset.

2) **Married couples have a joint credit report:** Your credit report is the one thing that remains separate when you join as one with your spouse. Although you and your spouse may secure loan accounts together, such as a car loan or mortgage, the accounts will show up on each of your individual credit reports. The payment history on joint accounts will impact both separate credit reports. However, your individual credit report is yours and yours alone.

3) **Your credit score measures your value as a person:** Although your credit score is a snapshot of your creditworthiness, it is not a depiction of your personal worthiness. We all endure financial hardships. These hardships are what we go through, not who we are. Refuse to equate your credit score with your personal worth.

4) **The better my job is, the better my credit score will be:** Your job title, job promotion, or your income have no impact on your credit score, and is not reported on your credit report. Remember, the goal of a credit report is to provide information on your credit and how you maintain your debt.

5) **Salary, child support, alimony, and other income affect my credit score:** The philosophy here is the same as explained in number 4. Your income, whether through your job or other means, has no impact on your credit score.

6) **Since I do not have any credit cards or credit card debt, I have a good credit score:** This myth is very popular and extremely misleading. As you will learn later in this book, your credit score consists of debt other than revolving credit such as credit cards. Your credit score reflects your payment history profiles how you manage debt.

7) **Only certain types of unpaid bills show up on my credit report and affect my credit:** Your creditors have the total discretion to report your paid and unpaid debts to whatever credit agency they choose. For example, if you have an unpaid hospital bill that has been lingering for years, the medical office has the right to report it to whatever credit reporting agency they see fit. I will discuss more about credit reporting agencies in a later chapter of this book.

8) **Asset accounts, such as checking, savings, and investment accounts, affect my credit score:** Again, remember that income does not impact your credit score. Your credit management and payment history affects your credit score.

9) **You only need to check your credit report if you know you have credit problems or do not pay your bills on time:** Credit champions are proactive. Credit champions respond to financial situations instead of reacting to them. Credit champions review their credit report frequently to monitor what lenders are reporting their information correctly.

Credit myths are not reality. They only become reality when you continue to feed your thoughts with them. You cannot become a credit champion if you embrace financial fantasies or credit myths. Truths about credit must prevail. Credit truths come when you are learn and are guided through understanding credit.

Credit myths can mire your ability to leverage your wealth. Credit myths can paralyze you from being proactive to fix your credit profile. Credit myths can stifle you from becoming financially healthy so you can increase your purchasing power.

Refuse to internalize the credit myths. Saturate yourself in learning the financial facts and how to rebuild your score. Once you move from a place of credit truths instead of myths, you can finally become a credit champion.

CHAPTER ACTIVITY

This chapter identified several credit myths that many individuals believe as the financial gospel. However, myths mess up your genuine ability to fix your money matters and correct your credit.

In the space provided, from the list of credit myths mentioned, choose those you have been actively living out. You can also list any credit myths not mentioned.

After you list each myth, briefly write how this has hindered you from being a credit champion. What are you going to do to act on the credit facts instead of the myths you have previously been living?

CHAPTER 4

Negative Credit Mindsets That Mess Up Your Financial Wellness

"Positive thinking will let you do everything better than negative thinking will."
- Zig Ziglar

Negative credit scores stem from negative mindsets about money, spending, and credit habits. It is often said, *"Wherever your mind goes is where your life goes."* Negative credit mindsets mess up your financial wellness. When you think wrong about your credit, it will never be strong.

There is a wide range of negative credit mindsets that individuals embrace that wreck their credit. On the financial website www.forbes.com, writer Molly Triffin identifies 8 negative mindsets that can affect your financial wellness. She says these mindsets become money-sabotaging emotions:

- **Guilt** – Guilt is a self-inflicted worry that you have done something wrong or have caused harm or embarrassment to another. When it pertains to financial guilt, oftentimes most people, especially women, tend to condemn themselves for having more than their friends, family members, and people in their community. As a result of this guilt, they waste money, loan money, and/or heavily contribute financially to organizations that put them in a financial quandary.

  Free yourself from the negative mindsets of financial guilt. Do not minimize your financial accomplishments because someone close to you has convinced you that your good financial position is an insult to those who are in a poor financial position. Refuse to allow financial guilt to create a credit catastrophe for you.

- **Regret** – Regret is when you are down on yourself for past decisions you made or did not make that could have positively altered your present set of circumstances. However, when you become paralyzed in regret, you will birth a victim mentality. This negative mentality will prohibit you from fixing what needs to be fixed for you to move forward. Credit champions may briefly battle with feelings of regret but they accept their past decisions, create a present plan of action, and have unyielding hope that their financial future will be better.

- **Anxiety** – Your upbringing, past experiences, and the current state of the nation's economy all contribute to your credit anxiety. Maybe your parents had unhealthy mindsets about money and credit that were transferred to you. Maybe you struggled to get out of debt previously and you have developed unnecessary stress for yourself because you walk on financial eggshells so you will not experience what you previously endured. Regardless of what has happened or is currently occurring, developing a realistic plan and sticking to it decreases your anxiety.

- **Jealousy** – This should be the number one reason why most individuals mess up their financial wellness. Yet, most people refuse to admit they are jealous. They mask their feelings and it is usually under the disguise of living beyond their financial means. Jealousy compels you to spend more than you have, to convince people you do not even know that you are on the same financial level as them.

  I must say the negative power of social media and its contribution create even more financial covetousness between people. Whether the blessings are authentic or not, the green-eyed monster continues to roar which causes already financially strapped people to create a deeper financial hole. Overcome the insecurities that prompt you to plunge into making unfavorable money decisions.

- **Sadness** – Oftentimes, life events such as death, divorce, and dismay engulf us with a cloud of melancholy emotions. The common response is to spend money, especially when there is an inheritance involved after death. Many believe spending excessively during difficult times makes them feel happier. Some people call it "retail therapy." However, this type of spending when you are sad results in overspending. Even during emotionally unhappy times, credit champions realize that sound financial spending decisions must occur.

- **Overconfidence** – People who are overconfident about their credit matters overestimate their financial abilities and portfolio. They tend to make lofty purchases and financial decisions. They ignore the financial realities of their present and do not plan for the unexpected money woes that may come. Overconfident people create a bigger financial hole for themselves.

- **Embarrassment** – Embarrassment about your debt and current financial mistakes is unnecessary. Why? First, your financial difficulties are nobody's business. Two, most of society, at one time or another, has been in a season of rebuilding their credit. Finally, you can get out of debt when you get out of the thought pattern that others are judging you because of your financial faux pas. Stop internalizing unconfirmed perceptions that people are condemning you about your negative credit. In actuality, nobody is probably watching your credit mistakes because they are consumed with their own troubles.

- **Feelings of being Overwhelmed** – When your money matters have negatively impacted your credit health and financial future it is definitely overwhelming, mounds of debt can scare anyone. It may shock you in a way that paralyzes you from pushing through your present financial chaos to a brighter stress-free financial status.

Regardless of the negative credit mindsets you have embodied, you can develop the opposite. As Zig Ziglar one quoted, *"Positive thinking will let you do everything better than negative thingking will."* Credit champions refuse to think negatively. They implement positive, prosperous, intentional, succinct, and consistent strategies that transform any level of financial struggles. Credit champions develop a disciplined financial lifestyle that manifests benefits.

How can you overcome guilt, regret, embarrassment, and the other negative credit mindsets? The first step is to **believe the best about yourself**. Understand that your credit report is not a report of who you are as a person. It is a snapshot of the financial decisions you made based on the knowledge, spending habits, and mindsets you developed. Remember, your bad financial decisions in the past does not make you a bad person in the present.

Secondly, **believe you can fix a poor credit score.** That is why you purchased this book. You are ready to rebuild what has been financially broken. Being positive and open-minded to learn, do the work, and change mindsets/financial habits will be the essential actions needed for you to progress from an unwanted credit score to a winning one.

Next, you must **identify and deal with the overspending triggers that are birthing credit chaos for you**. Maybe you overspend when you are sad. Or you may just live beyond your financial means because you are jealous, overwhelmed, or are trying to comfort your feelings of regret or guilt. Whatever is compelling you to overspend, identify it and deal with it head-on. Nothing in your life will be fixed when you avoid facing it.

Finally, **enlist a coach who can assist you in creating a clear and realistic plan for your financial future.**

Many people think that successful change is a solo endeavor. This could not be farther from the truth. When you examine the legendary champions of the world in their fields of expertise—tennis champions Serena and Venus Williams, basketball great Michael Jordan, and boxing icon Muhammad Ali—they all contribute their success to a coach, trainer, or team of people who taught them how to excel at their craft.

Credit champions who leverage their wealth and increase their purchasing power always have a knowledgeable coach in their circle. Whether paid or they donate their services, this coach is a voice of truth. They have walked a balanced path of financial hardship that turned into triumph.

A results-oriented coach does not coddle credit champions. They have a clear perspective that to train a champion who has sustainability, they must confront the habits that have stunted their financial growth. Champions need a clear and realistic regiment that develops the financial stamina and muscles needed to knockout those poor spending and payment history. You can change your financial future when you eliminate the negative credit mindsets and begin to think positively.

Many of my clients battle a plethora of additional unproductive credit mindsets such as fear, shame, and just simply not having a full scope of credit knowledge. On the other hand, credit champions work diligently to purge the undesirable mindset barriers to their financial wellness despite how many years they have embodied the negative mindsets. As you continue to internalize the information and strategies in this book, you will experience a mind shift and slowly grow into the credit champion you are destined to become.

CHAPTER ACTIVITY: Review the negative mindsets identified in this chapter. List the mindsets you have embraced. Beside each negative mindset, write a positive mindset you will adopt. Write a strategy for how you will eliminate your old negative mindset and embrace your new positive mindset.

SECTION 2:

CREDIT RESTORATION

"Don't be ashamed that you have bad credit. Be ashamed if you don't fix it."
–Anonymous

Now that you have received the basic credit education in section one, you are ready for the next phase of credit restoration. Credit restoration requires a commitment to unlearning and relearning credit information, honest self-reflection, and hard work. You cannot stop your progress by being ashamed of your poor credit. Be excited that you are on the pathway to fixing it.

By the end of this section, you will:

- ***Review your financial literacy assessment***
- ***Know the big 3 credit agencies and how to read your credit report***
- ***Understand what a FICO credit score is and why it is significant***
- ***Receive strategies for paying off debts and disputing incorrect accounts on your credit report***

There are no quick fixes when it pertains to credit restoration. It requires focus, a change of habits, and tightening your financial belt. Credit champions are always ready to endure regardless of obstacles and the hard work that it entails on the journey to credit restoration.

CHAPTER 5

Getting Financially Fit by Getting Financially Lit!—Completing Your Financial Literacy Assessment

"You can't get out of debt while keeping the same lifestyle that got you there."
–Dave Ramsey

As with any other area in your life, when you know better about credit you will do better with managing credit. Credit champions are willing to change their financial lifestyle by getting financially fit. Financial fitness begins with first becoming financially literate about your past, present, and future financial practices and strategies.

Financial literacy is the ability to understand and effectively implement personal financial management, budgeting, and investing. It is not a one-time event that repairs your poor credit. It is vastly more than that. Financial literacy is being committed to a lifestyle of continuous self-directed learning on basic key concepts such as budgeting, saving, how to manage and pay off debts, as well as set investment goals.

Becoming financially literate increases your ability to succeed at many life goals beyond the basics mentioned above. You can launch into activities such as saving for college education, retirement planning, high-yield investment activities, using debt responsibly, and running a business. Finally, the more financially literate you are, the less vulnerable you are to financial fraud activities.

Despite the perks and prosperity that it brings, as stated on www.investopedia.com, 66% of Americans are not financially literate. America has a huge financial literacy problem. Check out some shocking statistics below:

- **44% of Americans do not have enough cash on hand to cover a $400 life emergency**—The median out-of-pocket cost for an unexpected medical expense is $1,000, which means nearly half of our country is just one accident away from being hit with a bill they can't afford to pay.

- **43% of student loan borrowers are not making payments—**Tuition at public four-year institutions has increased by 213% in the past thirty years and nearly half of the twenty-two million Americans with federal student loans are either behind on payments or received permission to postpone payments due to economic hardship. Students need a better understanding of what repayment plans look like after graduation so they can make educated decisions about the degrees they are seeking.

- **33% of American adults have $0 saved for retirement—**56% of American adults have less than $10,000 saved for retirement when you combine the 33% who have nothing saved with the 23% who have a small amount saved. Most Americans will need at least $1 million to retire and millennials will likely need between $1.8 and $2.5 million. We are living longer lives, healthcare costs are constantly on the rise, pensions are a thing of the past, and the Social Security trust fund is on track to be depleted by 2034.

- **38% of U.S. households have credit card debt—**On average, they owe $16,048 with an APR of 16.47%. That means if they took 10 years to pay off their full balance, they would hand over $16,695 in interest to their card issuer, or more than twice what they initially spent. Most people are completely unaware they are paying so much in interest or that several strategies can reduce the amount of interest they pay significantly.

It is almost the common standard of society not to be knowledgeable about managing personal credit and money matters. Financially illiterate individuals are more prone to making poor spending decisions, piling on unnecessary and unsustainable bad debt, having bankruptcies, and housing foreclosures. All of these negative financial results stem from having the inability to have a clear financial perspective for long-term financial planning that actually generates favorable results.

To begin the journey of a financially fit and literate lifestyle, three terms always need to be swirling in your head: **need, want,** and **opportunity cost**. A **need** is something you **cannot** live without, i.e. water, food for fuel, and warmth. On the other hand, a **want** is something that is a luxury. If you do not have the item you desire, you will still manage to survive. Wants are things such as vacation, electronic gadgets, multiple pairs of shoes, a new purse, wristwatch, etc.

Opportunity cost is the cost of choosing one thing over another. It is what you miss out on when you choose one alternative over another. Opportunity costs are more than financial. They include time, sacrifice, effort, and emotional strength. When you are becoming financially fit and literate, you will have a healthy balance of purchasing needs versus wants. You will also clearly know the opportunity costs of your decisions and not create greater financial stress upon yourself.

Oftentimes, people in a credit crunch convince themselves, when making frivolous purchasing decisions, that what they are buying is a need because they are operating from a negative mindset. People with poor credit almost always purchase their *now* **wants** without truly having a plan to have the means for their future **needs**. But remember, credit champions happily delay temporary emotional thrills and frills to develop a sustainable wealth creation and increase their purchasing power.

CHAPTER SELF-CHECK: So, let's see how financially fit you are by completing a financial literacy assessment. Below are a series of questions about your personal financial management, budgeting, your understanding of credit, and other financial questions. Check the box that best answers the questions honestly. This assessment is not to judge or shame you. It is totally about determining where you are now to help you create a plan of growth.

CREDIT CHAMPIONS FINANCIAL LITERACY ASSESSMENT

	Yes	No
1. Do you have a checking account?		
2. Do you have a savings account that you contribute to regularly **and** do not withdraw from regularly?		
3. Do you reconcile your checking and savings account regularly?		
4. Is your monthly take-home income higher than your monthly expenses?		
5. Do you have a realistic budget that you are currently disciplined and committed to implementing monthly?		
6. Do you have overdraft protection on your checking account?		
7. Do you have at least two months or more of your monthly expenses saved in case something happened to your income?		
8. Do you have an emergency fund for unexpected repairs, incidents, and hospitalization?		
9. Does your savings account earn interest?		
10. Do you have an identity protection system in place?		
11. Do you pay your credit cards, installment loans, mortgages, and other bills on time?		
12. If you cannot pay your bills on time, are you proactive and call your creditors to schedule payment arrangements?		

	Yes	No
13. Do you know your FICO credit score shown on your credit report?		
14. Is your FICO credit score 740 or above?		
15. Do you review and monitor your credit report from the big three credit agencies every month?		
16. Is your credit report free of public record bankruptcies?		
17. Is your credit report free of collection accounts?		
18. Do you have a credit history that is free of multiple days of late payments?		
19. Is your credit utilization rate for your credit cards between 10%-30% of your total overall credit line?		
20. If you have a car, do you have current car insurance?		
21. Do you have homeowner's insurance if you have a house, or renter's insurance if you rent your housing?		
22. Do you have life insurance?		
23. Do you have all of the following: Last Will, Living Trust, Health Care Power of Attorney, and Financial Power of Attorney?		
24. Do you have all of your financial documents in one organized place so the appropriate people can easily access them if something were to happen to you?		
25. Do you have a realistic and active plan to decrease/eliminate your debt in a timely manner?		
26. Do you have a budgeting and debt-payoff tool system so you can create a clear financial plan?		
27. Do you have disciplined spending habits?		

	Yes	No
28. Do you file your federal and state taxes on time?		
29. Do you have a retirement fund that is separate from your job's retirement fund for you?		
30. Do you have a financial/credit coach to help guide you to understand what you do not know about finances so you can plan for your future?		

If you answered yes to **twenty-three** or more of these questions, you have a very good percentage rating for being financially literate. However, the goal is to strive to answer "yes" to all questions. So, you still have work to do if you did not answer yes to all questions. Understand that the goal of answering yes to all the questions is not desiring financial perfection, but it is working toward continuous progression.

Conversely, if you answered yes to less than **twenty-three** of these questions, you are positioning yourself for financial frustration and credit chaos. Also, you are leaving your family financially unprotected. Credit champions have a handle on their financial matters. They also plan for their future and leave their family in financial peace in case something happens to them. Credit champions are intentional and responsible both in their present and future finances.

CHAPTER 6

Credit Reporting Agencies: The Big 3 You Will Always See

"You control your credit score. Don't let your credit score control you."
-Anonymous

TransUnion. Experian. Equifax. These are the big three consumer credit reporting agencies. What do these agencies really do? These agencies are primarily responsible for monitoring your credit information.

They also assign your FICO score based on the five components. Let me be very clear. The big three credit bureaus **do not** control your credit score. The primary controller of your credit score is **YOU!**

Although the big three reporting agencies have the same purpose, each of their procedures may vary. According to www.msn.com, each agency may maintain different creditor information on you. Remember, the credit agencies receive information from lenders. All lenders may not share your payment history with all three agencies.

Also, they may share your information with all agencies but at different times. Also, when applying for credit, the lenders choose which credit agency to pull reports from. As a result, the number of credit inquiries differs, which creates a varying credit score. Finally, the big three may also give more weight to specific credit factors when calculating your score.

How Do I Read My Credit Report?

Every credit report, regardless of the agency delivering the report, always has five sections on it. Even if you have nothing to report in the section, it will still be present with no information. Below are the sections on your credit report.

1. **Personal information**—Includes your name, addresses, both current and past, as well as a place of employment.

2. **Credit summary**—This section includes all of the various types of current and delinquent accounts you have open. Accounts include revolving credit, real estate accounts, installment loans, other accounts, and collection accounts. Also, open and closed accounts, as well as the number of credit inquiries are listed in the credit summary.

3. **Account history**—According to www.balance.com, this section contains the bulk of the information. Collection accounts may appear in this section, but that depends on which credit agency is reporting. This section includes:

    - ***Creditor name***
    - ***Account number***
    - ***Account type***
    - ***Responsibility***
    - ***Monthly payment***
    - ***Date opened***
    - ***Date reported***
    - ***Balance***
    - ***Credit limit or loan amount***
    - ***High balance or high credit***
    - ***Past due***
    - ***Remarks***
    - ***Payment status***
    - ***Payment history***

4. **Public records** – Bankruptcy is the only public record in this section. Bankruptcies can stay on your report from seven to ten years.

5. **Credit inquiries** – This identifies all lenders who have accessed our credit report over the last two years. However, only hard credit inquiries are shown to lenders who access your account.

Oftentimes, your credit score will not be the same with each agency. However, the credit score range of **poor, fair, good,** or **excellent** is going to be the same for all agencies. I will explain the credit score ranges and why they are important to your overall financial wellness in the next chapter.

As you work to improve your credit score, understanding the big three credit reporting agencies will become a part of your financial lifestyle. It is important to review all three credit reports so you can get a clearer and more collective financial view. By law, you are to receive a free credit report annually. You can visit www.freecreditreport.com to do so. Conversely, credit champions do not mind paying a fee to receive their credit report more frequently. Monitoring what is on your report moves you closer to leveraging your wealth and increasing your purchasing power.

CHAPTER ACTIVITY

A) Visit www.freecreditreport.com and request your credit report from the big three credit agencies. Complete the below table so you can analyze your credit reports.

	Experian	**Transunion**	**Equifax**	**Comments**
Credit Score Number				
Credit Score Rating				
Accounts Listed				
Account History				
Public Records				
Credit Inquiries				

Additional comments:

____

____

____

____

____

CHAPTER ACTIVITY

B) Answer the below questions, based on your credit reports you pulled in Activity A listed on the previous page.

1) What was the credit score numerical differences on your three credit reports?

____

____

____

____

____

2) Were all of your accounts listed on all of your reports?

____

____

____

____

____

3) Was all the account information correct? (If not, please dispute the report. I will explain in a later chapter about disputes.)

____

____

____

____

____

4) After reviewing your credit report, explain what it tells you about your previous and current financial decisions. What are you going to change to better your credit history and score?

____

____

____

____

____

CHAPTER 7

The FICO 5 That Makes Your Credit Score Come Alive

"A credit score is a snapshot of an exact moment."
– Cate Williams

Despite how knowledgeable you are concerning credit, you still may be asking yourself, *What in the world is a FICO score?* FICO is an acronym for the legal business name called **F**air **I**saacs and **Co**mpany. According to https://en.wikipedia.org/wiki/FICO, the company was founded by two gentlemen, Bill **Fair** and Earl **Isaacs**, who created a credit scoring system in 1956.

Little did they imagine their first credit score system would be sold to about fifty American lending companies two years after they launched their company. Their FICO credit scoring system would become a worldwide fixture for how the financial industry lenders determine the potential creditworthiness of consumers. The FICO credit score ranges from excellent to very bad. They are outlined below, according to www.cafecredit.com:

- **Excellent: 800-850**
- **Very Good: 750-799**
- **Good: 700-749**
- **Fair: 650-699**
- **Poor: 600-649**
- **Very Bad: 300-599**

As you may realize, the higher your credit score the better your chances are to receive credit opportunities with low interest rates and better terms. If you are fortunate enough to score in the excellent or very good range, you can expect creditors to offer the lowest interest rates and the best terms. On the other hand, if you are in the poor or very bad range it will be very tough for you to receive credit. Usually, in these ranges, lenders see you as a very high risk and will only offer secured loans with high interest rates.

Secondly, how is your FICO credit score calculated? The experts at www.credit.com believe the following five components comprise your credit score. I will discuss each of the five components below.

Payment History

Your payment history is the record that demonstrates whether you make timely payments on your account. This accounts for **35%** of your total credit score. This category is the largest percentage of all the FICO components. So, it is critically important that you make every effort to pay your credit cards, installment loans, mortgages, as well as your finance company account on time.

How many times has one of your lenders tried to notify you and you have repeatedly ignored talking to them? Or, when you do answer the phone you are calm and willing to answer their questions as to why your payments have been late so they can help you? The true answer to these questions is more than likely that most people refuse to be proactive and cooperative with their creditors.

There are a vast number of reasons why individuals jeopardize creating a negative payment history. These reasons range from the following:

- **Embarrassment about having financial troubles**
- **Extreme frustration from having to talk about it**
- **Do not see a ray of hope of coming out of their financial hole**
- **Are unaware of the repercussions of a negative payment history being on their credit report**
- **Do not have the money or any hopes of getting the money in a timely manner to discuss payment arrangements**

Whatever the reasons, you must remember you are not alone if you are in a season of financial hardship. All of us fall on difficult times in which sometimes it becomes hard to make payments on time. However, please be confident in knowing that a large percentage of lenders truly understand when their clients fall on unexpected financial troubles.

Oftentimes, lending agencies are willing and ready to partner with you to negotiate payments that are a "win-win" situation. They would rather receive something instead of nothing. As a result, lenders are positioned to offer alternative payment plans if you are experiencing stressful money matters.

In conclusion, when it pertains to on-time payments as opposed to delinquencies, more weight is given to your payment history during the most recent twenty-four months. Strive to be proactive when you sense you may not be able to pay your creditors on time. Refuse to develop a negative credit payment history without communicating your circumstances to your lenders. Make sure you make timely payments or schedule payment arrangements to avoid a gloomy payment history.

Credit Utilization

Credit utilization is also called **debt usage**. This is only based on your revolving credit lines. It is the ratio between your credit card limits and the amount of your current credit balance reported.

The formula for calculating your debt usage is dividing your **total debt** by your **total available credit.** It is good to keep in mind that the ideal credit utilization percentage is to stay between **10% to 30%** of your overall total available credit line.

The component of credit utilization or debt usage encompasses **30%** of your total credit score. This is the second-highest percentage that creates your FICO score. The ideal percentage is to stay between 10% to 30% of your overall total available credit line. This ratio will fluctuate as you make credit purchases as well as pay your monthly credit card.

CREDIT UTILIZATION FORMULA

Credit Utilization = Your Total Revolving Credit Debit/Your Total Available Revolving Credit

According to www.experian.com/blogs, you can also calculate your per-card debt usage. To determine your per-card debt, the formula includes dividing your credit card balance by your total credit limit on the same card. When you are trying to get an honest snapshot of your credit wellness, it is better to monitor both your overall credit utilization and your per-card debt usage. To maintain a healthy credit utilization score, please know that credit card companies report your balances to the credit bureaus every thirty days.

As with your payment history, you can directly manage your credit utilization ratio. According to the financial experts via www.upgrade.com and www.experian.com/blogs, there are five strategies you can implement to have a healthier credit utilization rate:

- **Opening new credit accounts**
- **Pay down or pay off your credit card each month**

- **Requesting a credit limit increase from a credit card issuer**
- **Refinance multiple credit card debts with a personal loan**
- **Keeping open credit accounts that have zero balances, even if you don't intend to use them**

Being aware of your debt usage ratio helps you to continue to leverage your wealth and increase your purchasing power. Much like your credit score, credit utilization ratios have a range from being very poor to excellent.

To review, it is recommended that you keep your credit utilization rate between **10% to 30%** of your overall total available credit line. A higher ratio demonstrates that you may be experiencing financial difficulty. On the contrary, a lower credit utilization ratio tends to always increase your financial attractiveness to lenders.

Length of Credit

How long you have had credit and how old your accounts are. This calculates **15%** of your credit score. The key strategy for maintaining a healthy age of credit is to avoid closing your longest opened accounts unless necessary. When it pertains to your credit score, the age of your credit accounts is important and makes a huge impact.

Credit agencies examine the length your accounts have been not only opened but opened with positive activity. All of the ages of your accounts impact your score. From your oldest account to your newest account as well as the average length of all of your accounts are factors in calculating your credit score. Whatever the ages of your accounts, please strive to make timely payments.

Types of Accounts

The various types of credit accounts appearing on your credit report make up the diversity of your credit mix. This accounts for about **10%** of your credit score. It is wise to credit a good mixture of the accounts. The types of credit include installment loans, home equity loans, credit cards, and retail credit.

With every account that is listed on your credit report, the key to building your creditworthiness depends on your maintaining positive activity with your various accounts. In addition, on your various accounts, first practice maintaining small limits on revolving credit. Next, if at all possible, have a small installment loan amount. Finally, increasing your credit score requires you have positive activity with your secured credit cards as well as your rental payments.

New Credit

Comprising **10%** of your score is the number of times you have applied for various forms of credit in the past two years. A generally accepted rule of thumb when applying for credit, do not nonchalantly and haphazardly apply for new credit accounts. Open new credit accounts when you absolutely need it. Too many credit inquiries, especially in a short amount of time, make creditors suspicious of your credit character.

When fixing and rebuilding your credit, you should be strategic about the new credit you inquire about and take. You need to diversify your credit mix to enhance your credit score. If you are rebuilding your financial snapshot, new credit is impactful if you begin and keep a positive payment history.

Factors That Do Not Impact Your FICO Score but Influence the Lenders Decision

Below are several factors that do not impact your FICO score:

- Age
- Income
- Location
- Education
- Net worth
- Marital status
- Debit card use
- Criminal history
- Checking your own credit
- Whether you receive government benefits

Credit champions understand the power and significance of having a healthy FICO credit score. However, lenders examine other factors in addition to your credit score to make their decisions. According to www.scoresense.com, such factors include:

Income—Potential borrowers with little to no income will likely be viewed as a higher risk to creditors and might be denied. Reliable income automatically lets lenders know you have a source of repayment.

Employment —If you've worked at a company for several years or more, you can appear to be a good credit risk. If you have a history of moving from job to job, however, lenders might be concerned. This can result in credit denial or less favorable payment terms.

Down payment—The less money the lender loans, the less risk it assumes. If your credit score isn't that great, you can reduce the risk for the lender by offering a significant down payment. This might get you approved for the loan. On the other hand, if your credit score is good and you offer a generous down payment, you might be able to snag a lower interest rate.

Capital available—In case of a financial emergency, such as losing your job, lenders want to know if you have liquid assets on hand that can be used to pay your financial obligations. If you do, a lender may consider you less of a credit risk.

Length of time in your residence—The longer you've been in the same residence, paying either a mortgage or a consistent rent payment, the more stable and responsible you will appear to lenders.

Student loan debt—Because these types of loans can create a significant debt load, lenders may evaluate your risk based on them, especially if you are just out of college and haven't had time to firmly root yourself in your career.

Phone number stability—Just like living in the same house for a number of years can make you appear a good credit risk, so can having the same phone number. Both demonstrate stability. If you've changed your number repeatedly, however, it can give lenders reason to doubt your stability.

In closing, remember your credit score is a snapshot of a moment in time. Please do not fool yourself into thinking you will experience perpetual credit score highs. That is not true. There are always times of credit score highs, lows, and in-betweens. Yet, if you are currently in the season of rebuilding, do not dwell on beating yourself up about how you got there. Instead, work diligently to understand your credit, how to clean it up, and how each of the five FICO scores impacts your score.

Visual Representation of the FICO 5 Components That Comprise Your Credit Score

CHAPTER ACTIVITY: For this self-check session, use the credit reports you pulled in Chapter 6.

1. Review your credit history for the accounts listed on your report. Prepare a three-column chart. The first column should be the name of your accounts with negative payment history. The second column should list how many days you were late paying. Finally, the third column should be a brief explanation as to why you were late. The purpose of this is to reflect on your payment habits. Then to revise your payment habits. Finally, write a specific plan of how you will restart your payment history to be positive.

2. You learned in this chapter what credit utilization is and how to calculate it. In the space provided, calculate your per-card credit utilization as well as your overall credit utilization. Is your credit utilization between 10%-30% of your overall available credit line? If you answered no, which of the five strategies mentioned in this chapter will you implement for creating a healthier credit utilization rate?

CHAPTER 8

Paying Off and Disputing Your Debts

"We tend to focus on assets and forget about debts. Financial security requires facing up to the big picture: assets minus debts."
-Suze Orman

Leveraging your wealth and increasing your purchasing power includes more than just paying your bills on time. It requires working to drastically decrease or eliminate high debt. It is simple. The lower your debt, the higher your cash flow. The higher your cash flow, the more you have to save and invest. The more you have to save and invest, the more favorable and fluid your financial future will be.

Before I give you the strategies for paying off and disputing your debts, I will explain the various types of debts that are common. All of these types of debt listed below are listed on your credit report:

- **Secured Debt:** This is debt that requires collateral and an inquiry on your credit report. Collateral is an asset that you pledge if you default on your loan. If you do not have collateral, lenders may place a lien on the item you are financing. The lender has the authority to seize your collateral or repossess the item that has a lien on it should you not pay your debt. Examples of secured debt may include car loans, mortgage loans, and boat loans.

- **Unsecured Debt:** Debt that is not obtained for a physical item and does not require collateral is called unsecured debt. Higher interest rates oftentimes accompany this debt. As a result, if payment is repeatedly not received, lenders of unsecured debt tend to send the account to debt collection agencies or even file a lawsuit against you. So, when you are working to become financially healthy, paying off this type of debt first is best. Examples of unsecured debt are medical bills, student loans, personal loans, payday loans, and credit cards.

- **Revolving Debt:** Just like the word, revolving debt is an endless cycle of receiving a line of credit, paying it off to receive it again. The sneaky thing about this debt is that most individuals believe that paying the minimum required monthly payment suffices. Yet, in actuality, you are only paying the interest on your balance which will take a longer time to pay. Also, if you miss a payment, the lenders add a late fee as well as expect normal payment.

The debt that has an outstanding balance and has not gone into collections is known as **active debt.** If the amount of active debt you have is high, then tackle this with a plan before you jeopardize your credit standing by allowing these to go into collections status. Be proactive. If you are struggling to pay your debt on time, call your creditors to negotiate a short-term arrangement to decrease or skip your payment. However, this strategy should not become your normal. Credit champions negotiate alternative payment options when it is absolutely necessary. Those alternative options do not become their new payment strategy.

Credit champions are aware of and proactive in their actions. If they see that extra income is needed to meet their debt-payoff goals, credit champions are not prideful or embarrassed. They will do whatever they need to do to generate another stream of income to meet their financial needs.

There are several debt-payoff philosophies from various financial experts that people implement and have generated positive results. However, the bottom line is that you pay off your debt. First, you must **gather your debt data.** Listing all of your secured, unsecured, and revolving debt and the amounts are essential. Furthermore, you incur debt that is not necessarily from a lender but is something that needs to be paid in set amounts of installments. Examples include loans from family/friends or unexpected home repair paid directly to a company.

Next, **develop a timeline and strategy for paying your debts off.** Set a deadline for paying off each debt. Financial Freedom guru, Dave Ramsey, says the most efficient way to pay off your debts is done by what he calls the **debt snowball method.** Ramsey explains this methodology on his website, www.daveramsey.com. He explains, "*The debt snowball method is a debt reduction strategy where you pay off the debt in order of smallest to largest, gaining momentum as you knock out each balance. When the smallest debt is paid in full, you roll the money you were paying on that debt into the next smallest balance.*"

Thirdly, **examine the amount of income you have coming in**. Once you know how much you are working with, you can determine how much you are going to pay. It is at this step that you may decide if you should get a second job or create a plan for securing passive income to help pay your debt.

Next, **commit to tightening your spending.** Credit champions make the sacrifice of delaying gratification. It is at this stage that you must stick to only purchasing your needs and delay for a season buying your wants. You will be able to pay off your debt faster by adjusting your spending habits.

Finally, **try to pay a little bit more than is required.** Instead of paying the minimum monthly payment for your credit cards, pay a little more. It would be ideal if you were able to pay off the credit balance to save on interest. However, if that is not possible, focus on applying a little more than what is required and most importantly pay in a timely manner.

Debts That Go into Collections and How to Get Them Out

Sadly, oftentimes you may have debt that goes into collections. If this happens, you are not alone. As stated on www.daveramsey.com, *about seventy-seven million people had debt in collections.* When this occurs, it shows as a negative on your credit report. Also, depending on the debt collection agency, negotiating with them at this stage can be difficult but not impossible.

Debt collectors vary from being friendly and collaborative to working with you to resolve your collections to being extremely nasty and inflexible. Regardless, it is your goal to work with the collection agency to pay off your debt. Never ignore debt collection attempts because it is at this stage that you are very close to having your creditors sue you or putting a lien on your assets.

When your account has progressed to the collections stage, here are the steps to resolving your account:

- **Verifying the debt**—Don't assume your account that is in collections is automatically correct. You can ask for a debt validation and verification letter to ensure accuracy. For documentation purposes, keep all copies of written communication with the debt collector.

- **Negotiating the debt**—If you can't pay the full balance, a debt collector may be willing to negotiate. The agreement may be in terms of a partial payment or payment plan. Although, paying in full is truly the best move if it is financially possible for you to do so.

There are several scenarios you need to be aware of when negotiating a lump sum payment to a debt collector. One scenario is that they accept your offer. If this occurs, then you request they fax, email, or mail you a receipt once it is paid off. Make certain the receipt states the debt has been settled in full with the lump sum payment. It is easier and faster if payment is sent electronically. The receipt is sent quicker.

The second scenario is that they reject your offer. If this is the case, then ask the debt collector what amount of payment will they accept as paying off the account. When the debt collector tells you what their offer is and you accept, request a receipt stating debt has been paid in full.

Finally, if the debt collector representative is unwilling to negotiate, ask for another representative. Since most collectors receive a commission, some may be unwilling to budge due to their focus on receiving the largest commission possible. On the other hand, if another representative works with you pay, ask for a receipt, and move on. Whenever the debt is settled you should send a letter to all the credit bureaus to accelerate the process of the outstanding debt information being removed from your credit report.

- **Disputing the debt**—If you believe the debt is inaccurate, consider disputing it with the collection agency first. The agency provides the information that appears on your credit report, so if it is inaccurate, it will get corrected on your report in a timely manner.

Once you are at the stage where you have negotiated to pay off your debt collections, pay them off consistently until it has a zero balance. Beware of the threats debt collectors may use to intimidate you. Debt collectors **cannot** harass you at work if you have told them not to call. They **cannot** call your friends and relatives to bully you into paying. Debt collectors can call and leave a message with friends and family you have put down as references. However, they **cannot** reveal any information about the call. Lastly, they **cannot** threaten to send you to jail if payment is not rendered.

Credit champions have learned to implement a balance financial philosophy when it pertains to debt and assets. They work diligently to minimize their debt ratio and increase their assets. When in debt, credit champions do not ignore it. They negotiate and pay it off. Sacrifice and transparency about what their financial picture reveals play key roles in leveraging their wealth and increasing their purchasing power. Credit champions live by this financial equation: **assets minus debts equals financial wealth and wellness.**

CHAPTER ACTIVITY: Before you begin to negotiate to pay off your debt, create a debt payment schedule. Use your credit reports to list both your active debt and the debt you have in collections. Determine how much you can afford to pay monthly and what date it will be paid off. Use the chart below. Remember, it may be beneficial to use the **debt snowball payoff method** that was discussed in this chapter.

Name of creditor	Amount owed	Minimum monthly payment	Number of months it will take to pay off	Date it will be paid off	Is this active debt or is it in debt collection?

SECTION 3:

CREDIT ELEVATION

"What you choose to do with your money shows if you are powerful or powerless."
-Suze Orman

Section 1 gave you basic credit education. Section 2 focused on credit restoration. In this last section, I will discuss ways you can experience authentic credit elevation.

In this section, you will learn:

- ***Embracing the budgeting lifestyle***
- ***The 5 ways to build and boost your credit***
- ***The 5 keys to financial wealth***
- ***Protecting your credit character***

Suze Orman once quoted, *"What you choose to do with your money shows if you are powerful or powerless."* You have received the education about how to successfully comprehend how having favorable credit leverages your wealth and expand your purchasing power. You have the most efficient tools and the best industry information you need for credit restoration. Now, it is time to literally put your money where your mouth is.

Are you truly ready to repair your credit? Are you ready to tighten your budget belt and slash your unnecessary spending? Do you want to face the truth about what your credit report states and put in the work to make the improvements? Are you ready to clean up your credit character and build the wealth you have been talking about for years, yet never did anything to change it?

If you have made it to this part of the workbook, then you are steps closer to becoming the credit champion you desire. Anything in life worth having is worth the intense and intentional work required to manifest results. You can fix your credit so you can leverage your wealth and have a consistent cash flow to increase your purchasing power.

There is no turning back at this point. You have come too far to quit now. You have received the mandatory credit education. You are well on your way to experiencing credit restoration. The final stage is to unleash your inner power to do everything required to ascend to the levels of unending credit elevation.

CHAPTER 9

Embracing the Budget Lifestyle

"A debt problem is, at its core, a budgeting problem."
–Natalie Pace

BUDGET! Sadly, this word puts a bad taste in the mouths of many people. It is often viewed in a negative connotation. It is continuously thought of as a means of negative control. **BUDGET!** In reality, a budget is not a negative but it is the positive pillar that produces sustainable financial wellness.

Natalie Pace, the author of *The ABCs of Money*, declares that at the core of all debt problems is a budgeting problem. When current statistics show that 1 out of 10 Americans is being pursued by debt collectors it is extremely important to embrace the lifestyle of budgeting, especially when you are one of the people being pursued by debt collectors. Budgeting is what closes the gap between your financial dreams and your actual reality.

Budgeting is not a one and done strategy. It is a lifestyle that will help you get off of the financial intensive care unit. A relevant and realistic budget will breathe new life into your life.

Budgeting helps you to control your spending because you have a visual reminder in your budget spreadsheet. You become more in tune with whether you are spending money on what you need or what you want. As you develop a new spending appetite, you will become aware of your purchasing decisions. In a nutshell, a budget can help curb your spending that is impulsive, emotional, and unnecessary.

Budgeting helps you get out of debt. As you are strategic and succinct about paying off your debt, you will notice that you have more cash flow. Credit champions do not view the extra cash as something they can quickly spend on frivolous wants. To a credit champion, extra cash flow equates to more money to save, invest, and place in an emergency fund.

Finally, adopting a lifestyle of budgeting simply demonstrates proper financial management. Credit champions are astute at credit and money management. They do not sit back and allow their finances to dictate their lifestyle. On the contrary, having a financial blueprint of your income and expenses brings peace, freedom, and flexibility. A budget keeps you from feeling overwhelmed and anxious.

Before You Create Your Budget

You understand that a budget is important. Now, you are ready to proceed to begin your new lifestyle as a budgeter. Before you dive into creating your budget, answering the below questions is essential:

- **Where does my money come from?** – Know what income you have consistently coming in and if you should generate additional income.
- **Where does my money go?** – Identifying where your money goes supersedes far beyond just paying creditors. When you create a budget, you must list how much you spend monthly to live. This includes expenditures such as gas for your car, insurance (car, life, homeowner's/renter's insurance), entertainment, and food. You must be transparent about where you spend your money.
- **What are my bills, what is the total amount, what are the monthly payments, and when are they due?** – This is an outline of your secured debt, unsecured debt, revolving credit, and, if applicable, debt collections. You should also identify household bills such as water, phone, light, and gas bills.

Budget Creation

You can research sample budget templates or electronic software applications to decide what works for you. They range from simple to elaborate. On the next page is a sample of a very simple budget sheet.

MONTHLY INCOME/EXPENSE BUDGET

Total Monthly Income:				
Expense	**Due Date**	**Budget Amount**	**Actual Amount**	**Total**
Rent/Mortgage				
Gas/Oil				
Electric				
Water/Sewage				
Phone				
Life Insurance				
Car Insurance				
Taxes (if not included in mortgage)				
Homeowner's/Tenant Insurance (if not included in mortgage)				
Installment loan with ____________				
Installment loan with ____________				
Charge Account _______________				
Charge Account _______________				
Charge Account _______________				
Charge Account ______________				
Charge Account ______________				
Food-Grocery Store				
Auto expenses				
Gasoline/Transportation				
Medical (doctor, dentist, eye care, prescriptions)				
Daycare				
Lunches/snacks, coffee, etc.				
Cable TV				
Pay per view, video rental				
Dry cleaning, laundry				
Education expenses (including books)				
Church/religious donations				
Other donations				
Pet expenses				
Barber/hair salon				

Total Monthly Income:				
Expense	**Due Date**	**Budget Amount**	**Actual Amount**	**Total**
Allowances (including children)				
Cigarettes/beverages (including alcoholic)				
Newspaper/magazines, etc.				
Entertainment (including babysitting expense)				
Fast Food				
Clubs, sports hobbies				
New clothing/shoes				
College Funds				
Gifts-Birthdays, anniversaries				
Gifts-Holidays				
Emergency Savings				
Saving for ________________				
Other Expenses				

________________________ - ________________________ = $________________

Total Net Income **Total Expenses** **Total Net Income**

CHAPTER ACTIVITY: Answer the three questions under Before You Create Your Budget. Then research the internet for **FREE** budget templates or budget software. Prepare a realistic and relevant budget you can implement immediately. Then stick to it at least for thirty days without any excuses, after which you can examine and determine if your budget needs to be revised.

CHAPTER 10

The Keys to Leveraging Your Financial Wealth and Increasing Your Purchasing Power

"When money realizes that it is in good hands, it wants to stay and multiply in those hands."
–Idowu Koyenikan

The law of attraction is a philosophy that declares that we can attract whatever we focus on. Focus is in word and action. Credit champions attract wealth by first believing that wealth creation can be a dream realized. Then they put the steps in motion to transform their dreams into an actual reality.

Below are essential keys to leveraging your financial wealth and increasing your purchasing power.

- **Desire wealth** – Desire is a wish, a craving, and a want. There is a proverb that says, "as a man thinks in his heart, so is he." When in your heart you truly crave wealth, you will be more committed to the process of obtaining it. Nothing will be too difficult. Nor will the wait will not seem long because your desire will outweigh your distractions.

- **Your relationship with money** – Yes, you have a relationship with money, whether you believe it or not. Examine your relationship with yourself and others. Ask yourself are these relationships healthy or unhealthy? The relationship that you have with yourself and others is the same type of relationship you have with your money.

- **Protection** – Financial protection is the foundation of wealth building. Life insurance, homeowner's insurance, and car insurance are a few ways that you can protect your assets.

- **Multiple streams of income –** Financial experts believe that wealthy people on average, have seven streams of income. They have learned that diversification and creating multiple streams of income is the key to sustainable wealth creation. Credit champions are not quick to leave their jobs because of professional frustration. On the contrary, credit champions understand that having a job with consistent income is pivotal to experiencing financial freedom.

There are several ways to have multiple streams of incomes:

- **Investments**
- **Get a part-time job**
- **Birth an income-generating business**
- **Turn your passion or hobby into a profit**
- **Write a book and create online courses to teach life skills**

As you rebuild and boost your credit and decrease your spending, you will develop a budgeting lifestyle toward financial wealth. Decreasing your spending will increase your cash flow. Increasing cash flow leverages your financial wealth and purchasing power. To achieve all of this is to work toward leveraging your financial wealth and increasing your purchasing power.

CHAPTER SELF CHECK: Below, outline how you can create at least five streams of additional income. Create a simple timeline for ensuring your streams of income. Remember that multiple streams of income are a common characteristic of wealthy individuals.

CLOSING

Continuing the Credit Conversation: Protecting Your Credit Character

"Money, like emotions, is something you must control
to keep your life on the right track."
–Natasha Munson

You have made it! You have learned and unlearned important information about becoming a credit champion. However, your journey does not end. It truly has just begun.

At the beginning of this book, I started the credit conversation about how critical it is to fix your credit character. As we end this book, I will focus on eight activities that will protect your credit character so your wealth and purchasing power can continuously grow. These activities include:

- ***Credit building***
- ***Credit restoration***
- ***Credit maintenance***
- ***Credit sustainability***
- ***Estate planning: Wills and Trusts***
- ***Budgeting and savings***
- ***Financial coaching***
- ***Personal investment***

Credit building

Credit is a large part of your financial power. Yet, as I have stated in the book, dealing with not having a credit history at all is much easier than restoring your credit. To build credit, taking out a small loan such as a credit card or a car loan is the best step. When you receive your first loan, make your payments on time each month, and try to pay the loan off early. Let me repeat this important point —**it easier to build credit than to restore it**!

Credit restoration

If you are one of the 30% of Americans who, unfortunately, has fallen into a financial predicament that has negatively impacted your credit history, you can restore it. It will be difficult but credit restoration is doable. Remember, a low credit score does not mean you will not be able to obtain a loan or credit card so that you can rebuild your credit. A low credit score equates to having a high interest rate.

Your negative credit history does not mean you are forever losing your financial power. It is just a huge warning sign that you need to implement financial lifestyle changes. Examining your spending habits that impact your debt payment habits and then making the necessary adjustments is key to credit restoration.

Credit maintenance

After you have worked hard to restore your credit, you need to maintain the positive changes that resulted in increasing your credit score. This is where you start protecting what you worked hard to change. Credit maintenance entails increasing your financial discipline that requires you to keep your credit score and credit character on the upswing.

If you have ever worked hard to lose weight, it required that you eliminate your unhealthy eating, implementing healthier food choices, and consistently exercising your body. After you lose the weight, you know that to maintain your new weight loss and a healthier lifestyle will require you to continue the same strategies that helped you lose the weight. To keep your status as a credit champion, you must continue the same routines and financial decisions that allowed you to restore your credit. Old habits will generate old results. New habits generate new results.

Credit sustainability

Credit champions become true masters of ensuring their credit sustainability. Credit sustainability focuses on meeting the needs of the present without compromising the resources allocated for their future. It compels people to frame financial decisions in the long-term rather than on short-term gains. Credit sustainability is a future-focused mindset that implements present-day strategies that will generate and maintain increasing financial gains over a long period of time.

Estate Planning: Wills and Trusts

It has often been said that you cannot take your money and other possessions with you when you die. On the other hand, it is fiscally responsible to have your assets allocated to designated people when you are no longer on this earth. Credit champions realize the importance of estate planning.

If you do not have instructions about what happens to your estate when you die, the government will have a plan. Their plan seldom includes sharing your estate with your loved ones. So, it is best to be financially responsible and implement a plan that includes having a will and a trust.

A **will** is a legally binding enforceable document stating how you want your affairs handled and assets distributed after you die. Your will places your decisions in the hands of the judge presiding over your estate transfer. In the absence of a will, your estate will be transferred to **probate court** to distribute your assets after debts have been paid.

On the opposite end, a **trust** is a fiduciary relationship in which you give another party authority to handle your assets for the beneficiaries you have named. Trusts are more detailed than wills. For trusts to be legally valid, it must identify the trustor, the trustee, the successor trustee, and the trust beneficiaries.

A **trustor** is an individual or organization that gifts funds or assets to others. This is the person who has left their assets in a trust. The **successor trustee** or also known as the **executor** of the trust is responsible for managing your trust and its assets. The **trust beneficiaries** the individual or group of individuals for whom a trust is created.

Budgeting and savings

Budgeting has been discussed in this book. It is important to realize that budgeting is not a one and done activity. It is not something to do to reach your financial goal. Budgeting is a lifestyle. To maintain consistency in your financial freedom, budgeting is a continuous activity in your life

Your budget is not just something to ensure that you pay bills and get out of debt. It is a visual means of knowing where your money is being allocated. Savings should be a standard category on your budget worksheet. Financial experts suggest that the standard rule is to save at least **10%** of your income. Eventually, as you decrease your debt and increase your cash flow, you can grow to save from **20%-30%** of your income.

Financial coaching

Success is a team endeavor. However, you must ensure that you have the right team around you who not only talks their talk but has walks their walk. When seeking a financial coach, they must have several solid, evident characteristics.

According to www.investingwithoutexperts.com, there are six characteristics that you should inquire about from the financial coach that you are seeking to enlist as you begin your journey to financial freedom. First, the financial coach must have **personal experience living out solid money principles.** How can you coach someone that you have not lived out yourself?

Secondly, the coach you are soliciting should have **confidence as a result of financial success.** Success births confidence. Thirdly, all coaches especially one who is dealing with money management should possess the genuine **heart of a teacher.** Teachers educate, engage in the learning process with students and they empower students with the skills and resources they need to master the content being taught.

Next, **financial coaches should be continuously involved in financial/money management training and certification.** The coach guiding you should know current financial industry practices and knowledge. Another characteristic is for them to have a **passion for the topic of personal finances.** Finally, your financial coach should demonstrate across life settings **trustworthiness.**

Personal investment

You have paid off your high interest debt – **Check!** You have a credit score that is in the very good or higher range. – **Check!** You have at least three to six months of your living expenses in an account that can be liquidated easily. – **Check!** You are discipline and actively implementing your financial budget without unhealthy spending habits. – **Check!** Now, it is time for you to start investing.

Credit champions have grasped the fact that investing has tremendous wealth-building benefits. It allows you to put your money in financial activities that have the potential to earn strong rates of return. On the other hand, investing has huge risks. You can potentially lose your money as you have the opportunity to gain profit as well.

Yet, wise investments can cancel out the risk of losing money. But the opportunity to gain can generate a lucrative return that you would have otherwise missed out on had you not invested in the first place. When you are striving to leverage your wealth and increase your purchasing power, investing your money should always be written in your long-term financial plans.

I completely understand the psychological battle you may endure once you have worked hard to rebuild your credit and develop a lifestyle of not spending your money frivolously. However, investing your money is not haphazard spending. It is disbursing money with the intentional purpose of seeing a return on your money.

When you are beginning your investment journey, it is best to start with low-risk activities. Before you invest your dollars, learn about investments from a financial investment coach, books, or financial groups. The financial experts via www.bankrate.com identify several low-risk investments that are great options for beginning investors:

- **Preferred stock**
- **Savings bonds**
- **Corporate bonds**
- **Money market funds**
- **Certificates of deposit**
- **Dividend-paying stocks**
- **High yield savings accounts**
- **Treasury bills, notes, bonds, and TIPS**

In closing, you can become a credit champion with the determination to fix what is contributing to your negative credit character. Next, you must develop an unwavering discipline. You must unlearn unhealthy spending habits, negative credit mindsets, and misleading views you have towards money. Being disciplined to tighten up your financial budget and decrease your debt by any means necessary will push you closer to becoming a credit champion.

Finally, dedication to your new financial journey is essential to leveraging your wealth and increasing your purchasing power. You did not get into debt overnight, and you will not become financially free overnight. Becoming a champion of your credit and your financial wellness is not a quick process either. It is a journey. A journey that will pay off if you do not quit.

As you close this book, please know that you are not ending the conversation about your credit. Continuing your personal credit conversation entails continuing your credit and wealth-building journey. When you feel as though the path is too difficult, recall these statistics:

- An estimated 30% of Americans have poor or bad credit scores—www.foxbusiness.com
- One in every eight Americans are completely unaware of their current credit score—www.nypost.com

- The NFCC study found that 36% of people think there's no reason to check their credit score. About 8% didn't know how to, and another 8% thought it's too expensive—www.creditdonkey.com
- 44% of consumers believe that credit scores and credit reports mean the same thing—www.creditdonkey.com
- 41% of Americans do not understand that a credit score measures your risk of not paying a loan—www.creditdonkey.com

You are on your way to being a credit champion. You did not read this book and complete the activities **not** to become victorious in your quest for financial wellness. Believe that you can do this! Implement the tips and strategies suggested in this book without excuse or delay! Find an accountability coach who will be honest, gentle yet firm with you as you take this new journey. Revisit the qualities you should look for in the financial coach.

You are ready to become a credit champion! You are set with all the tools that you need to become a credit champion! Now just go unleash the credit champion that you desire to become.

CHAPTER SELF CHECK: The beginning chapter quote by Natasha Munson says, *"Money, like emotions, is something you must control to keep your life on the right track."* Credit champions cannot achieve their new financial goals if they do not have the mindset of a credit champion.

Below are mantras from www.gobankingrates.com and www.girlboss.com about money, debt, and credit that will help you believe that you can achieve the financial goals you have set. Recite a mantra each day that you are working diligently to become a credit champion.

MANTRAS ABOUT MONEY, DEBT, and CREDIT

- I Am Financially Free.
- I Am A Money Magnet.
- I Must Stay Out of Debt.
- Money Flows Freely to Me.
- I Can Become A Money Master.
- I Need to Save More, Spend Less.
- I Need to Re-Prioritize My Spending.
- Control My Money, Control My Life.
- My Great Ideas Can Make Me Rich.
- I Naturally Attract Good Fortune.
- My Income Exceeds My Expenses.
- My Income Increases Constantly.
- I Am Wealthy in More Ways Than One.
- I Choose to Live a Rich and Full Life.
- I Can Look at My Finances Without Fear.
- I Am Worthy of All the Richness I Desire.
- I Give Myself Permission to Prosper and Grow.
- My Job/Business Allows Me to Live the Life I Desire.
- I Am Connected to The Universal Supply of Money.
- Making More Money Doesn't Have to Be Hard.

- I Need to Sustain Wealth — Not Just Make Money.
- My Financial Freedom Starts with A 'B' For BUDGET.
- I Deserve to Be Paid for My Skills, Time and Knowledge.
- There Is Always More Than Enough Money in My Life.
- Every Dollar I Spend and Donate Comes Back to Me Multiplied
- I Have the Power to Create the Success and Build the Wealth I Desire.
- I Have A Positive Relationship to Money and Know How to Spend It Wisely.
- I Am Grateful for The Abundance That I Have and The Abundance on Its Way.
- **I Release All Resistance to Attracting Money. I Am Worthy of A Positive Cashflow.**

SAMPLE FORMS, LETTERS, and WORKSHEETS

In this section are forms, letters, and worksheets to help you on your journey to becoming a credit champion.

CREDIT CLARITY REFLECTION SHEET:
How Did I Get in A Credit Crunch?

1) What does my having a favorable credit report and history really mean to me?

2) What positive things did my parents/guardians teach me about money management and credit management?

3) What negative things did my parents/guardians teach me about money management and credit management?

4) What are some things that I need to unlearn about money management and credit management?

5) **What are some things that I need to learn about money management and credit management?**

6) **In two to three sentences, write your personal commitment statement to keep you focused on your new journey of becoming a credit champion.**

CREDIT SCORE GOAL SETTING SHEET:
Where Do I Go and Grow with My Credit?

Complete the below table to get a clearer picture of your credit score goals.

1) What is my current credit score and rating for the following?

Date ____________________

Experian ____________________ Credit Rating ____________________
Transunion ____________________ Credit Rating ____________________
Equifax ____________________ Credit Rating ____________________

2) What credit score would I like to increase to within 3, 6 and 12 months? (Please be realistic with your credit score increase.)

3 months: Date ____________________

Experian ____________________ Credit Rating ____________________
Transunion ____________________ Credit Rating ____________________
Equifax ____________________ Credit Rating ____________________

6 months: Date ____________________

Experian ____________________ Credit Rating ____________________
Transunion ____________________ Credit Rating ____________________
Equifax ____________________ Credit Rating ____________________

12 months: Date ____________________

Experian ____________________ Credit Rating ____________________
Transunion ____________________ Credit Rating ____________________
Equifax ____________________ Credit Rating ____________________

3) Using the information shared in this book, identify the steps you will take to ensure you achieve your credit score goals.

____
____
____
____
____

4) **Identify two to three people you can trust to be your accountability partners for improving your credit score.**

DAILY EXPENSE TRACKER
Week 1

Track your daily spending on this worksheet to see exactly where your money is going. Do this for seven straight days. Then determine if you are spending more on your needs or your wants. If your wants are more than your needs, develop a strategy for not succumbing to your wants and sticking to taking care of your needs.

Date	Expense	Amount	Need or a Want?

DAILY EXPENSE TRACKER
Week 2

Track your daily spending on this worksheet to see exactly where your money is going. Do this for seven straight days. Then determine if you are spending more on your needs or your wants. If your wants are more than your needs, develop a strategy for not succumbing to your wants and sticking to taking care of your needs.

Date	Expense	Amount	Need or a Want?

DAILY EXPENSE TRACKER
Week 3

Track your daily spending on this worksheet to see exactly where your money is going. Do this for seven straight days. Then determine if you are spending more on your needs or your wants. If your wants are more than your needs, develop a strategy for not succumbing to your wants and sticking to taking care of your needs.

Date	Expense	Amount	Need or a Want?

DAILY EXPENSE TRACKER
Week 4

Track your daily spending on this worksheet to see exactly where your money is going. Do this for seven straight days. Then determine if you are spending more on your needs or your wants. If your wants are more than your needs, develop a strategy for not succumbing to your wants and sticking to taking care of your needs.

Date	Expense	Amount	Need or a Want?

DAILY EXPENSE TRACKER
Week 5

Track your daily spending on this worksheet to see exactly where your money is going. Do this for seven straight days. Then determine if you are spending more on your needs or your wants. If your wants are more than your needs, develop a strategy for not succumbing to your wants and sticking to taking care of your needs.

Date	Expense	Amount	Need or a Want?

DAILY EXPENSE TRACKER

Week 6

Track your daily spending on this worksheet to see exactly where your money is going. Do this for seven straight days. Then determine if you are spending more on your needs or your wants. If your wants are more than your needs, develop a strategy for not succumbing to your wants and sticking to taking care of your needs.

Date	Expense	Amount	Need or a Want?

MONTHLY INCOME/EXPENSE BUDGET

Total Monthly Income:				
Expense	**Due Date**	**Budget Amount**	**Actual Amount**	**Total**
Rent/Mortgage				
Gas/Oil				
Electric				
Water/Sewage				
Phone				
Life Insurance				
Car Insurance				
Taxes (if not included in mortgage)				
Homeowner's/Tenant Insurance (if not included in mortgage)				
Installment loan with ____________				
Installment loan with ____________				
Charge Account _______________				
Charge Account _______________				
Charge Account _______________				
Charge Account ______________				
Charge Account ______________				
Food-Grocery Store				
Auto expenses				
Gasoline/Transportation				
Medical (doctor, dentist, eye care, prescriptions)				
Daycare				
Lunches/snacks, coffee, etc.				
Cable TV				
Pay per view, video rental				
Dry cleaning, laundry				
Education expenses (including books)				
Church/religious donations				
Other donations				
Pet expenses				
Barber/hair salon				

Total Monthly Income:				
Expense	**Due Date**	**Budget Amount**	**Actual Amount**	**Total**
Allowances (including children)				
Cigarettes/beverages (including alcoholic)				
Newspaper/magazines, etc.				
Entertainment (including babysitting expense)				
Fast Food				
Clubs, sports hobbies				
New clothing/shoes				
College Funds				
Gifts-Birthdays, anniversaries				
Gifts-Holidays				
Emergency Savings				
Saving for ________________				
Other Expenses				

______________________ - ______________________ = $______________

Total Net Income **Total Expenses** **Total Net Income**

SAMPLE DISPUTE LETTER

When mailing your dispute letter to a creditor, send your letter by certified mail, "return receipt requested," so you can document that the credit reporting company received it. Remember to include copies of the applicable enclosures and save copies for your files.

(Your Name)
(Your Address)
(Your City, State, Zip Code)

(Date)

Complaint Department
(Company Name)
(Street Address)
(City, State, Zip Code)

Dear Sir or Madam:

I am writing to dispute the following information in my file. I have circled the items I dispute on the attached copy of the report I received.

This item **(identify item(s) disputed by name of the source, such as creditors or tax court, and identify the type of item, such as credit account, judgment, etc.)** is **(inaccurate or incomplete)** because (**describe what is inaccurate or incomplete and why)**. I am requesting that the item be removed **(or request another specific change)** to correct the information.

Enclosed are copies of **(use this sentence if applicable and describe any enclosed documentation, such as payment records and court documents)** supporting my position. Please reinvestigate this **(these)** matter**(s)** and **(delete or correct)** the disputed item**(s)** as soon as possible.

Sincerely,

Your name

Enclosures: **(List what you are enclosing.)**

(NOTE: You may search the Internet to find other free sample dispute letters that may fit you.)

CREDIT CHAMPION 30-DAY SUCCESS JOURNAL

As you begin your new journey to becoming the credit champion you were destined to be, I suggest you journal your experience for thirty days. Expert studies show that journaling helps you to focus more on your goals and increases your success rate.

You will be unlearning and learning a tremendous amount about yourself and who you are becoming. Take a few moments each day for thirty days to chronicle your new journey of rebuilding your credit, increasing your credit score, and creating a healthier financial life.

Credit Champion Journal

Day # ______________

Date ______________

Credit Champion Journal

Day # ______________

Date ______________

Credit Champion Journal

Day # ______________

Date _______________

Credit Champion Journal

Day # ______________

Date ______________

Credit Champion Journal

Day # ______________

Date ________________

Credit Champion Journal

Day # ______________

Date ______________

Credit Champion Journal

Day # ______________

Date _______________

Credit Champion Journal

Day # ________________

Date __________________

Credit Champion Journal

Day # ______________

Date ______________

Credit Champion Journal

Day # ______________

Date ______________

Credit Champion Journal

Day # ______________

Date _______________

Credit Champion Journal

Day # ________________

Date ________________

Credit Champion Journal

Day # ______________

Date _______________

Credit Champion Journal

Day # ______________

Date ______________

Credit Champion Journal

Day # ______________

Date ______________

Credit Champion Journal

Day # ______________

Date ______________

Credit Champion Journal

Day # ________________

Date __________________

Credit Champion Journal

Day # ______________

Date ______________

Credit Champion Journal

Day # ______________

Date ______________

Credit Champion Journal

Day # _______________

Date ________________

Credit Champion Journal

Day # ______________

Date ______________

Credit Champion Journal

Day # ______________

Date ______________

Credit Champion Journal

Day # ______________

Date ______________

Credit Champion Journal

Day # _______________

Date ________________

Credit Champion Journal

Day # ________________

Date _________________

Credit Champion Journal

Day # ________________

Date ________________

Credit Champion Journal

Day # ______________

Date _______________

Credit Champion Journal

Day # ______________

Date ______________

Credit Champion Journal

Day # ________________

Date _________________

Credit Champion Journal

Day # ______________

Date ______________

Made in United States
North Haven, CT
05 November 2026

21766943R00067